WEDDING
PAPERCRAFTS

LARK
New York

An Imprint of Sterling Publishing
1166 Avenue of the Americas
New York, NY 10036

ISBN 978-1-4547-0922-0

Distributed in Canada by Sterling Publishing
c/o Canadian Manda Group, 664 Annette Street
Toronto, Ontario, Canada M6S 2C8
Distributed in the United Kingdom by GMC Distribution Services
Castle Place, 166 High Street, Lewes, East Sussex, England
BN7 1XU
Distributed in Australia by Capricorn Link (Australia) Pty. Ltd.
P.O. Box 704, Windsor, NSW 2756, Australia

For information about custom editions, special sales, and
premium and corporate purchases, please contact Sterling Special
Sales at 800-805-5489 or specialsales@sterlingpublishing.com.

Photography by Christopher Bain
Template illustrations by Orrin Lundgren
Step-by-step illustrations by Sue Havens
Design by Lorie Pagnozzi

Manufactured in China

2 4 6 8 10 9 7 5 3 1

WEDDING
PAPERCRAFTS

*Add Handmade Charm
to Your Celebration*

LARK
New York

CONTENTS

INTRODUCTION

A wedding is the ultimate form for a couple's mutual expression of their love for each other. What better way to infuse the celebration with your uniquely combined personality, charm, and style than by creating and displaying your own handmade wedding papercrafts?

It's no wonder that paper is one of the most popular crafting materials—it provides endless creative opportunities! Paper is relatively inexpensive, easy to work with, and, best of all, you can easily achieve impressive, beautiful, and elegant results. There are myriad variations in paper's color, texture, and weight. It is a tremendously versatile artistic medium.

The beautiful wedding papercrafts included in this book are all customizable. Choose colors of paper materials to match your wedding's color scheme; make the Recycled Book Pom-Pom Flower Bouquet (page 67) using pages from an old book by an author you both love; make the Make-Beautiful-Music-Together Centerpiece (page 20) with sheet music from your first-dance song. The opportunities for adding charm, warmth, and personality to your wedding with these projects are endless.

Doing these projects provides a creative outlet during the hustle and bustle of the wedding-planning process. Plus, you can involve your family and friends, making the preparations and the wedding itself even more special.

Create the lovely craft items in *Wedding Papercrafts* and enjoy a one-of-a-kind wedding celebration you'll remember for a lifetime.

BASICS

The following pages include information on the basic materials and tools as well as tips and techniques to help you create interesting, personalized crafts for your wedding celebration.

PAPER & TOOLS

While most of the projects in this book specify which paper and materials to use, there are certain core items that are essential to a crafter's arsenal.

PAPER

An assortment of cardstock, tissue paper, regular copy paper, transfer paper, and tracing paper, plus papers of assorted patterns and textures are all good to have on reserve. Use cardstock to create boxes or the body of a lantern, as it's sturdy and holds its shape. Tissue paper is wonderful for creating paper flowers and decorative overlay accents on cards, but it is also very delicate. With so many variations in the strength, weight, and texture of paper, it's best to stick to the particular paper listed for a project, if specified.

TOOLS

Craft Knife ∗ Craft stores sell a variety of craft knives. Some have spongy handles for extra comfort and traction, while others are very basic. Try out a few to gauge your preference before starting a paper-cutting project. Be sure to have extra blades at hand, as a sharp craft knife blade is essential for creating intricate and accurate cuts.

⁂

TIP: If you've never worked with a craft knife before, we recommend practicing before you begin a project. Start by cutting a variety of shapes from an assortment of papers. The pressure and movement of the blade differs depending on the texture and weight of the paper, and it's best to practice to get your bearings before beginning the actual project.

⁂

Cutting Mat ＊ Use a self-healing cutting mat to protect your workspace surface. These are available in a variety of sizes. If you don't have a self-healing mat, a regular one will do just fine.

Scissors ＊ A pair of sharp craft scissors is an invaluable crafting tool. You can use them for everything—from cutting open the packaging of a roll of tissue paper, to cutting out the template for a project. Scissors are a must-have craft-kit item.

Bone Folder ＊ A bone folder is a smooth-edged, flat hand tool used to fold and crease paper materials.

Steel Ruler ＊ A steel ruler is best for projects in which a craft knife is used. The craft knife

blade runs smoothly along the edge of the ruler, resulting in a neater, more accurate cut. Craft knives can dig into the edge of a plastic or wooden ruler, causing snags and scratches that can result in imprecise cuts and measurements.

Adhesives ＊ It's always good to have a couple different adhesives on hand for any craft project. You'll need a variety of adhesives to create the projects in this book. A glue gun (plus a packet of glue sticks) is handy for gluing cardstock or other paper where a strong, quick-drying adhesive is needed. Tape is handy for holding pieces of paper in place as you work on them, and standard craft glue is always good to have around.

EXTRAS

Craft stores and websites are full of neat gadgets and tools. Don't be afraid to experiment with any that catch your eye. Here are a few extra tools that may come in handy:

Hole Punches ＊ Hole punches are available in a ton of fun designs, patterns, and motifs. Use them to add extra decorative flair to any paper project.

Decorative Scissors ＊ Add elaborate borders to your crafts in just a few snips. From simple zigzag patterns to more intricate designs, these scissors offer an easy way to add elegance to your papercrafts.

USING THE TEMPLATES

Each template notes the percentage at which they should be copied from the book to be rendered at full size for the project. Here are some ways to transfer templates to the paper for each project:

Copy the template from the book on to regular copy paper * Place the copy over the paper you are using for the project, and use the template as a cutting guide. Or, alternatively, cut the shape from the template on the copy paper to create a stencil. Lay it down on your project paper and use a pencil to trace it onto the paper.

Use transfer paper * Lay the transfer paper on top of the project paper, and then position the template on top of that. Using a pencil or tracing stylus to trace the shape, press the template design onto the project paper. The transfer paper backing—usually graphite or charcoal—will transfer the template design onto the project paper.

Trace the template * Using a dark pencil, charcoal pencil, or other transferrable marking tool, lay the template marked side down on the project paper and rub the back of the template to transfer the design to the paper.

SAFETY TIPS

Take your time! Crafting is a fun, creative, and often meditative and calming activity. Take pleasure in the process. Go at your own pace, avoid distractions, and enjoy! You're much less likely to make mistakes or hurt yourself while crafting if you're relaxed and focused on the project at hand.

Make a point to be aware of the position of your hands and fingers before each cut. Always hold the paper with your hands behind the scissors or craft knife blade.

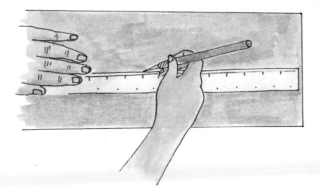

Use a cutting mat. Make sure that your work surface is stable and uncluttered, and that the mat will not slip.

Be sure to cover your craft knife's blade with its plastic cover when it is not in use.

SOME TIPS BEFORE YOU BEGIN

CUSTOMIZING YOUR PROJECTS

The projects in this book are all customizable. You can use them as a springboard, and add your own unique spin to the wedding crafts presented. Use papers that match the color scheme of your wedding; don't be afraid to play with different textures or patterns.

INVOLVE FAMILY AND FRIENDS

Often, family and friends of the wedding couple can't wait to help and be involved in the preparations for the big day. These wedding papercrafts provide the perfect opportunity! Have your bridesmaids come over for a crafting session. Have family members of both the bride and groom work together on a project. Or, simply invite some of your favorite people over for a crafting party. You'll feel productive through this creative outlet, and your family and friends will feel great getting in on the action and contributing to the celebration in such a meaningful and inclusive way.

DECOR

Tissue Paper Rose Decorations

DESIGNER: VALERIE LLOYD

These tissue paper roses make beautiful centerpieces when displayed in clusters. They are made out of inexpensive materials, and can be made assembly-line style with the help of family and friends. For an evening display, a flameless LED tealight can be inserted into the hollow center of each flower to turn the roses into glowing luminaries.

MATERIALS & TOOLS TO MAKE ONE TISSUE PAPER ROSE

- Leaf template (page 94)
- Petal template (page 95)
- 9-inch (22.9 cm) paper plate
- Scissors
- Glue gun
- Low-temp hot glue sticks

- Four sheets of pink tissue paper
- One sheet of yellow tissue paper
- Empty toilet paper tube
- Flameless LED tealight (optional)
- One sheet of green tissue paper

Instructions

1. Use scissors to make five evenly spaced cuts toward the center of the paper plate to create five sections that are connected in the middle. These cuts should be approximately 3½ inches (8.9 cm) long. Apply a 1-inch (2.5 cm) bead of hot glue along the left side of a cut near the outer edge of the plate. Take the section just to the right of the cut, and pull it to the left, overlapping the left section by about 1½ inches (3.8 cm) . Press down over the glue bead, and hold until the hot glue solidifies. Do the same for the other four sections, until the plate resembles a steep-sided bowl B.

2. Use the petal template to cut out 24 to 30 petals from the pink tissue paper. The tissue can be cut in multiple layers to make cutting the petal shapes faster.

to hold the top of the petal against it. Attaching this row of petals at both the top and bottom will ensure that the paper plate is entirely hidden by petals. Affix the next petal in the same way, just to the right, and slightly overlapping the first petal. Continue adding petals all the way around the circumference of the paper plate. Once the plate is completely covered, add a second row of petals, this time just attaching the base of the petals **D**.

4. Now begin adding a row of petals to the inside of the paper plate. To do this, place a dot of glue at the base of the petal, on its back side rather than its front **E**. Press down inside to affix it to the

3. Take a petal, and gather the base of it to form a gathered point. At the same time, grasp the top edge of the petal and bend it outward **C**. Apply a dot of glue to the base of the petal on its front side and adhere it to the outside of the paper plate. Add a dot of glue to the top of the outside of the paper plate,

paper plate. The first row inside should also be tacked with glue at the top to completely hide the paper plate. Add a second row inside by affixing the petals toward the center of the plate. The rose should be full enough once the interior of the plate is completely covered by petals.

5. Cut a 4 x 24-inch (10.1 x 60.9 cm) strip of yellow tissue paper. Cut a fine fringe along one side of the length of the strip, cutting about halfway through the width of the strip. The simplest way to do this is to fold the strip in half several times to cut through multiple layers at once. Cut a 1-inch (2.5 cm) ring off the end of the empty cardboard toilet paper tube. Use hot glue to affix one end of the fringe strip to the cardboard

ring, lining up the smooth side of the strip with one end of the ring. Wrap the fringe around the ring as many times as it will go, until the end of the fringe strip is reached. Seal the end with a dot of glue. Ruffle the fringe to make a messy pouf that covers the center of the ring.

6. Insert the yellow-fringed pouf into the center of the rose. For a luminary rose, place a flameless LED tealight inside the rose first, and then slide the fringed center over it. Use the leaf template to cut out green tissue paper leaves. These can be glued to the underside of the rose, or just arranged on a table with more tissue paper rose decorations.

Paper Wisteria Branches

DESIGNER: KATHRYN GODWIN

Inspired by beautiful, lush cascades of wisteria vines, this unique backdrop is a statement piece that will add simple elegance to any wedding venue. Hang this backdrop at your ceremony or reception to add a whimsical touch to your celebration.

MATERIALS & TOOLS

- Cardstock paper in any color (We used white)
- Hole punches, ¾ (1.9 cm) and 1½ inches (3.8 cm)
- Scissors
- Hot glue gun
- Hot glue sticks
- Branches (You can gather these from outside and save on buying them at a store)
- Cotton twine

Instructions

1. Gather 20 thin branches or sticks from outdoors. Focus on finding ones that are about ¼– ½ inch (0.6–1.2 cm) in diameter, and range in length from 10–30 inches (25.4–76.2 cm) or more.

2. Punch ¾-inch (1.9 cm) and 1½ inch-(3.8 cm) circles from cardstock. Depending on branch lengths, plan to use 10 to 20 of each size per branch.

3. Cut a slit halfway into each of the circles **A**.

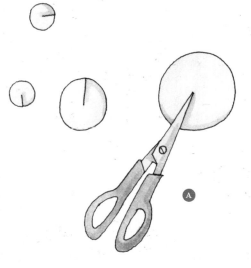

4. Starting at the tip of the branch, pull a ¾ inch (1.9 cm) cut circle around the branch. If the branches are thicker, there may be a need to cut a little hole at the center of a circle to help it form around the branch **B**.

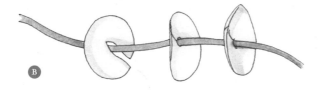

B

5. Apply a dot of hot glue and pull the cut ends of the circle to slightly overlap and close around the branch. This will create a small cone shape; make sure all cones face down to the branch's tip.

6. Work up the branch, adding ¾-inch (1.9 cm) circles, spacing them about 1–1½ inches (2.5–3.8 cm) apart. At the midpoint of the branch, switch to the 1½-inch (3.8 cm) circles, using the same spacing.

7. Use the cotton twine to tie a knot ½ inch (1.2 cm) from the end of the branch. Wrap around several times, and then double knot the twine. Decide how low to suspend the branches, and leave enough twine attached to allow them to hang at different lengths, creating an interesting cascading effect. Lay the branches out on the floor to help decide placement and order before stringing and suspending.

Cascading Butterflies

Cascading Butterflies

DESIGNER: JESSICA FEDIW

Adorn chairs with a cascade of paper butterflies to make an elegant statement at your wedding reception.

MATERIALS & TOOLS

- Butterfly templates (page 96)
- 30 sheets of white copy paper, 8½ x 11 inches (21.6 x 27.9 cm)
- 10 yards of gold 20-gauge beading wire

- Transparent tape
- Wire cutters
- Needle-nose pliers
- Scissors

Instructions

1. Take one piece of copy paper, fold it in half, and then unfold. Fold in each side to the middle fold. Fold in half one more time. There will be two folds on one side and one fold on the other **A**.

A

2. Trace a butterfly template on the side with two folds. Trace as many as can fit.

3. Cut out the traced butterflies. There will be two butterflies for each cut.

4. Continue to repeat Steps 1–3, cutting out many of each size of butterfly.

5. Use the wire cutters to cut one 55-inch (137.9 cm) piece and two 48-inch (129.2 cm) pieces of beading wire. Place the three wires together and match at one end. Wrap one wire around the other two using the needle-nose pliers. Turn in the ends to prevent them from catching on anything. Curl the other wire ends with the pliers.

6. Tape the butterflies onto the wire. For a gradual effect, tape more of the larger ones toward the bottom, more medium-size ones in the middle, and the smallest ones at the top.

7. Arrange on one side of a chair and secure with tape.

TIP: If using thin paper, cut out more butterflies at a time. Do Step 1 for two pieces of paper. Then do Step 2 on one of those. Stack the two pieces together, matching up the sides with the two folds, and cut out the butterflies.

Make-Beautiful-Music-Together Centerpiece

DESIGNER: SANDI GENOVESE

This three-dimensional centerpiece folds flat for convenient storage after the big event, but makes a spectacular display by simply pulling the front cover around to meet the back cover. Secure it with the heart-shaped clips and the ribbon tied into a bow.

MATERIALS & TOOLS

- Sheet music of couple's favorite song
- Cream cardstock, five 6 x 9-inch (15.2 x 22.8 cm) pieces, five 6-inch squares, and five strips measuring 1¾ x 7 inches (4.4 x 17.8 cm)
- Red, black, green, and gold-striped paper
- Adhesive of choice
- Photograph of a champagne bottle
- Approximately 10 inches (25.4 cm) of 1/8-inch (.32 cm) satin ribbon
- Heart-shaped clips
- Red ink pad

This type of construction is called a five-pointed star book. It's made up of five identical sections, each comprised of three layers (a front, a middle, and a back).

Instructions

1. Trim sheet music to 6 x 9 inches (15.2 x 22.8 cm). Back it with cream cardstock to add thickness and fold it in half to create the back layer.

2. Cut a strip of cream cardstock 1¾ x 7 inches (4.4 x 17. 8 cm). Fold it in half to make the middle layer.

3. Cut three hearts from the red paper. Fold one in half and attach it to the middle of the strip (aligning the fold lines). Attach the other two hearts on both sides of the folded heart.

TIP: You can add detail to the hearts with a stamp and watermark ink pad.

4. To create the front layer, cut a 6-inch (15.2 cm) square from cream cardstock. Mark a 4½-inch (11.4 cm) square window in the center. Fold the front layer in half and cut out the window opening.

5. Embellish the front layer with "XOX" and the date cut from the black paper. Add a champagne bottle made from pieces of the gold, black, green, and red paper.

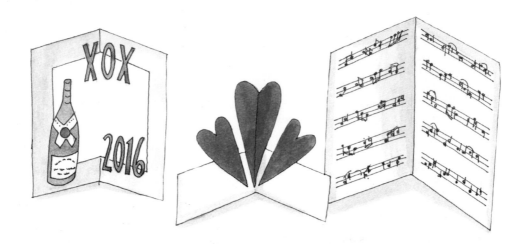

TIP: Take a photo of a champagne bottle and use the photo as a pattern.

6. Attach the three layers together along the side edges with an aggressive adhesive.

7. Repeat Steps 1–6 four times for a total of five completed sections. Create the five-pointed star book by attaching the front of one section to the back of the next section until all five are fastened together.

8. Cut two pieces of cream cardstock to 4½ x 6 inches (11.4 x 15.2 cm). Decorate one as the front and one as the back cover of the book. Embellish the front cover with a 2-inch (5.1 cm) strip of gold-striped paper, a quarter inch strip of red paper, a heart, and the date. The heart on the back cover is created by combining fingerprints from the bride and the groom by having them each press a finger in the red ink pad and then press down on the paper so they overlap into a heart shape.

9. Tape a 12-inch (30.5 cm) length of ribbon to the front and a second ribbon to the back of the book; then attach the front and back cover over top.

10. Add a heart-shaped clip to the front cover and one to the back cover to aid in holding the book open.

Vellum-Cut Window Lantern

DESIGNER: BRITA VALLENS

Create elegant lanterns with cut vellum windows to add a warm glow to reception tables. Follow the pattern using the template provided, or create your own design.

MATERIALS & TOOLS

- Lantern body template (page 97)
- Window design template (page 98)
- One large sheet of colored cardstock
- Five sheets of matte-translucent vellum (reserve one for practice)
- Craft knife

- Cutting mat
- Pencil or other marking tool
- Metal ruler
- Eraser
- Hot glue gun
- Hot glue sticks
- Bone folder

Instructions

1. Use the template provided to cut the lantern body from the piece of cardstock. Be careful to cut the outline of the lantern body only, and use the cutting mat to protect your work surface.

TIP: If you plan on placing Christmas lights instead of LED tealights inside the lantern, be sure to cut the square piece labeled "Christmas light port" on the bottom section of the lantern body template.

2. Use your ruler to fold the cardstock along the dotted lines marked on the template. Position the ruler along each folding line, then pull the cardstock up against the ruler to create the fold. Use a bone fold to make the folds crisp.

3. Set the lantern body aside, and make four copies of the design template for the vellum window. Lay one piece of vellum over one of the design template copies, and cut the vellum following the design on the template. Repeat this step for each of the sheets of vellum. Take your time, to ensure neat cuts and to avoid tearing the vellum.

TIP: If you've never used a craft knife, you may want to practice on the extra piece of vellum before you begin the project, to become familiar with the feel of the vellum and to perfect your technique. Or, you can use decorative hole punches—available in a variety of shapes—to punch shapes out of the vellum to avoid using a craft knife.

4. Use the bone folder to sharpen the folds, which will make up the lantern's four sides, bottom, and tabs.

5. Apply glue along the outermost edges of each of the vellum pieces and position them in each window on the backside of the lantern body piece.

6. Use your hot glue gun to construct the box. Make sure the tab pieces are glued and folded into the inside of the box .

7. Place a large LED-powered tealight (use a few LED tealights in the lantern if they are small) or Christmas lights inside the lantern.

Ⓐ

Paper Flower Branch

Paper Flower Branch

DESIGNER: KATHRYN GODWIN

The joining of elements from nature with paper has always been fascinating. This combination of a discarded tree branch with paper flowers from delicate coffee filters creates a romantic and unexpected scene. This charming piece can be used as a centerpiece lying flat on a table, clustered as branches in a vase, or suspended as a chandelier.

MATERIALS & TOOLS

- Half petal template (page 99)
- Coffee filters
- Fabric dye (orange, fuchsia, yellow)
- Scissors
- 20-gauge floral wire
- Wire cutters
- Tacky glue
- Paintbrush
- Branch
- Hot glue gun
- Hot glue
- Plastic Tarp

Instructions

1. Mix the fabric dye with water in small bowls or buckets to desired colors. The more water, the lighter the color will be, and mixing colors like orange and fuchsia will create a coral hue.

2. Dip coffee filters, individually, into the dye, set on a plastic tarp, and allow to dry for a day.

TIP: If you do not have a plastic tarp handy, lay the dyed coffee filters on a plastic trash bag or a cookie pan covered with tin foil to dry.

3. Once dry, fold each coffee filter in half. Fold it in half twice more; the coffee filter is now folded in eighths.

4. Use the half petal template to cut along the single folded side of each coffee filter 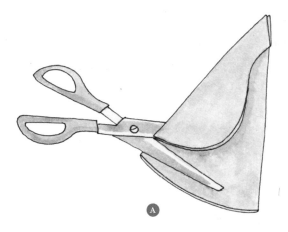. Open the filter up; there will be four petals attached to each other. Four of these pieces are needed for each flower.

6. Apply beads of tacky glue to the coffee filter and smooth it out with a finger or paintbrush to the edges of the petal.

7. Press a second petal piece over the glue and smooth it flat. Allow time to dry, then trim any edges that aren't smoothly aligned.

8. Pinching each petal between your thumb and first two fingers, begin to form a soft curve to each petal. The wire helps the curved petal to hold its shape .

5. Lay a single petal piece flat on a table. Cut two pieces of floral wire to fit inside the width of the petal. Set as an "X" within the petal .

9. For the center petals, curve them until the ends come together in almost a ball or bud shape. For the outer petals, allow them to have a subtle curve, but remain mostly flat.

10. Choose a brighter color dyed filter and fold it in half. Trim 1 inch (2.5 cm) off the edge and cut it into quarters.

12. Using hot glue, attach the bud to the outer petal layer. Be sure you don't align the petals on the layers; rather, offset the petals.

13. Find the smoother/flat parts of the tree branch and apply hot glue. Attach each flower and hold until the glue sets.

11. Pinch at the center of the quarter and glue into the center of the flower bud ⓓ.

TIP: Working in odd quantities (five, seven, nine) of flowers creates the most dynamic composition.

Heart-Shaped 3-D Decoration

DESIGNER: KIMBERLY BART

Hang this playful decoration from the ceiling of your ceremony or reception venue, use it to adorn a welcome table, or cut a slit in the side of the heart to create a box for gift envelopes. Have wedding guests use colored markers to cover the heart with wishes for the newlyweds.

MATERIALS & TOOLS

- Heart template (page 100)
- Black pen
- Scissors
- Tape measure
- Masking tape
- Hot glue gun
- Hot glue sticks
- Forty 7½-inch (19.0 cm) paper doilies

- Two sheets of cardboard measuring 32 x 24 inches (81.2 x 60.9 cm) (alternatively, disassemble a box of 18 x 18 inches [45.7 x 45.7 cm] or larger from which you can cut the 32 x 24-inch sheets).
- 36 inches (91.4 cm) of twine or ribbon

Instructions

1. To cut the two sheets measuring 32 x 24 inches (81.2 x 60.9 cm) from a box (must be a box 18 inches square or larger): Disassemble the box so it lies flat on the table. Starting at one corner of the cardboard, cut two sheets measuring 32 x 24 inches (81.2 x 60.9 cm). Set aside the leftover large scrap pieces for use later in this project.

2. Trace the heart template onto one sheet of the cardboard. Using scissors, cut out the first heart.

3. Lay this heart on top of the second sheet of cardboard. Trace, then cut, the second heart. Set aside the two hearts.

4. Gather the large scrap pieces of cardboard from Step 1, and cut four strips, 32 x 3½ inches (81.2 x 8.9 cm).

5. Fold one strip of cardboard into a "V" shape. Tape the tip of the "V" to the edge of the point of the heart Ⓐ.

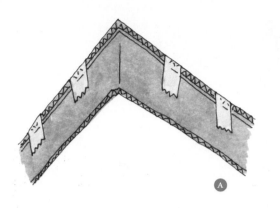

6. Use the side of a pen to form or curl the two strips of cardboard to make it more malleable as you shape the strips around the heart form.

7. Continue taping the cardboard to the edge of the heart until the entire heart has a strip around it ⓑ.

8. Cut a 4 x 4-inch (10.1 x 10.1 cm) square of cardboard from a piece of scrap. Cut two 1-inch (2.5 cm) slits in the square and wrap the twine around it, leaving 12 inches (30.5 cm) of each end loose.

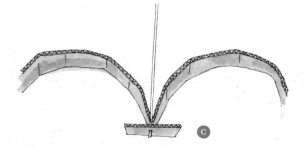

9. Cut a ¼-inch (.63 cm) hole in the top center portion of the heart. Thread the twine or ribbon through the hole from the inside of the heart to the outside. Tie a knot at the top of the heart and place some hot glue on the hole to seal it in place ⓒ.

10. Place the second heart on top of the heart with the taped sides already in place. Tape the second heart piece all the way around the edges to complete the 3-D heart form ⓓ.

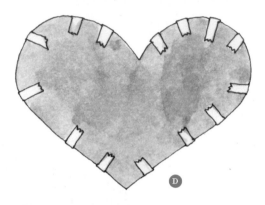

11. Using your glue gun, glue the paper doilies to the heart form, layering them from the bottom up, until the entire front and back portions of the heart are covered. Be sure to allow the doilies to hang off the sides a bit so they can be folded over the edge. Fold the edges down the sides and glue them.

12. Cut the leftover doilies in half. Using a glue gun, glue the half doilies on the sides of the heart, covering any exposed cardboard.

Paper Ball Backdrop

Paper Ball Backdrop

DESIGNER: JESSICA FEDIW

Create a unique, colorful, and inexpensive backdrop for your celebration venue. These paper balls are fun and easy to make.

MATERIALS & TOOLS

- 12 x 12 inch (30.5 x 30.5 cm) cardstock
- Scissors
- Ball templates (page 101)
- Sewing machine, sewing

- machine needle, and thread, or tacky glue
- Hot glue gun
- Hot glue sticks
- Clear monofilament fishing line

Instructions

1. Use ball templates and cut out four to six circles for each ball you are making.

2. Fold each circle in half and unfold. Stack the circles together, folds aligned.

3. Sew down the middle fold, making sure to backstitch at the beginning and end. If sewing is not an option, put a line of tacky glue on each fold in between each circle. Allow the glue to thoroughly dry.

4. Repeat Steps 1–3 as many times as needed.

5. Cut one 65-inch (165.1 cm) length and eight 75-inch (190.5 cm) lengths of fishing line.

6. Tie loops on each end of the 65-inch (165.1 cm) length, which will be used for hanging. Then, tie each of the eight longer pieces onto this hanging wire. Spread them out evenly and use the hot glue to secure them in place.

7. Lay out the circles and decide their placement on the hanging wire structure you created in Step 6.

8. Fold open each outer circle of a ball. Using the glue gun, add a thin line of glue down the middle of one side. Hold that circle closed in half until the glue dries. This will help the ball keep its shape.

9. Add a thin line of glue to the fold on the other side of the ball and place on the fishing line. Make sure the line is in the glue and then hold the circle closed until the glue dries.

10. Repeat Steps 8 and 9 for each ball. Trim off excess fishing line and open up all the balls until your desired fullness is achieved.

Paper Leaf Garland

DESIGNER: KATHRYN GODWIN

This exquisite paper leaf garland can be constructed with wire for a stiff, structured yet pliable table runner, or with jute to allow for swags or draping over an arbor for the ceremony or along a banister in an entry hall. Use this piece to highlight a special element of your celebration in a sophisticated and elegant way. Instructions for both of the varieties are detailed below.

MATERIALS & TOOLS

- Leaf template (page 102)
- Cardstock or scrapbook paper: three shades of solid green; linen textured may be used
- Scissors
- Green cloth–wrapped floral wire
- Jute twine
- Hot glue gun
- Hot glue sticks
- Crepe paper, one sheet in cream

Instructions

1. Use the leaf template to cut out the leaf shapes. Create 8–10 leaves per each cluster along your garland. Fold each leaf in half lengthwise to create dimension and a center vein.

FOR A STIFFER STRUCTURE, SUCH AS A TABLE RUNNER:

1. Apply a dot of hot glue at the stem and wrap it around the floral wire. Begin to work down the wire branch, clustering 8–10 leaves at slightly different angles, and alternating paper colors for each leaf. Fold the excess stem around the wire and hold while the glue cools 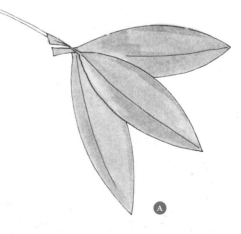.

2. To create longer pieces of garland with wire, hook pieces of the wire together to create a chain **B**.

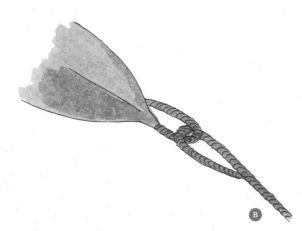

angle.) Vary the paper color you use for each leaf **C**.

3. For every two leaves that are glued at an angle on the underside of the jute, apply a leaf to the top side to cover the glue and jute. Create a section of five to eight leaves, and then skip 3 inches (7.6 cm) of string before attaching the next cluster of leaves. This will allow for the swagging and draping motion of the garland **D**.

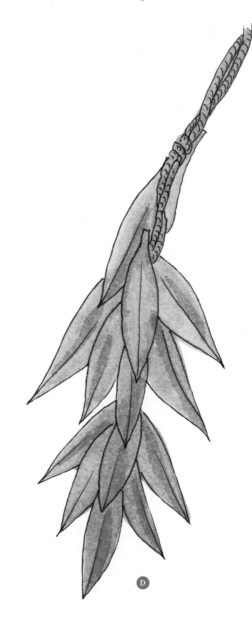

FOR A SOFT GARLAND TO ALLOW FOR SWAGS AND DRAPING:

1. Measure a length of the jute to the desired span of the garland. Double string the jute and knot it together every 6 inches (15.2 cm); this provides extra strength for hanging or suspending.

2. Apply a dot of hot glue to the stem and hold to the underside of the jute. Allow about 1 inch (2.5 cm) of spacing between leaves, and attach at slight angles. (**NOTE:** Applying glue along the side of the leaf edge will help to secure it to the string at an

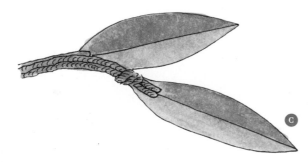

4. Work in from both ends and join the leaves at the middle by overlapping and tucking. This will create a center point from which the leaves will seemingly grow as they extend outward.

TO MAKE THE BERRIES:

1. Cut 2-inch (5.1 cm) squares from the crepe paper. (These do not have to be perfectly measured.)

2. Begin to fold the corners into the center, for each square, until a little ball is formed from the continual folding.

3. Tuck the paper berries into the leaves, securing with a dot of hot glue to the underside of each.

TIP: To create an unexpected and more romantic element, tuck real flowers into the garland. The mixing of paper with natural textures creates a lovely setting.

Paper Flower Pom-Pom

DESIGNER: BRITA VALLENS

There's a reason paper pom-poms are one of the most popular party decorations: they're inexpensive, easy to make, and create a beautiful effect. Use tissue paper in a variety of colors and hang these decorations with clear monofilament for a whimsical addition to your wedding decor. Invite family and friends over for a fun paper pom-pom-making party and you'll have tons of these pretty decorations in no time!

MATERIALS & TOOLS

- One package of tissue paper, ten sheets, 20 x 20 inches (50.8 x 50.8 cm) per flower

- Scissors
- Monofilament
- Glitter spray paint (optional)

Instructions

1. Unfold 10 tissue paper sheets so they lay in a flat stack. Fold the stack of sheets in half to create a fold in the center.

2. Cut the stack in half along the fold to double the number of sheets.

3. Combine the two stacks to create one stack of 20 sheets of tissue paper. Starting at one of the short ends of the rectangle, fold the stack up in an accordion fold. Press down on the tissue paper as you make each fold, so the folds will be easy to see.

4. Open the sheets and lay them flat in a stack so the accordion folds are visible.

5. Refold the tissue paper five sheets at a time to create thinner paper accordions. Trim the edges of the tissue paper accordions so they are rounded; these will be the textured "petals" of the flower pom-pom. Repeat this step for the next four sets of tissue paper sheets Ⓐ.

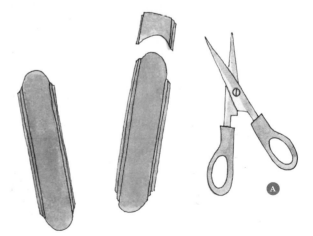

6. Put all of the sets of accordion folds together in a stack (they should now all have rounded edges), and tie the stack together in the middle with the monofilament. Be sure to cut the monofilament long enough to create a loop at the top for hanging B.

motion. Take your time as you pull each layer of tissue paper out to avoid tearing. Hold the pom gently between your knees to stabilize it as you gently pull the paper layers outward. When all of the layers have been pulled out, fluff the individual "petal" sections to shape the pom-pom into a neater circular shape D.

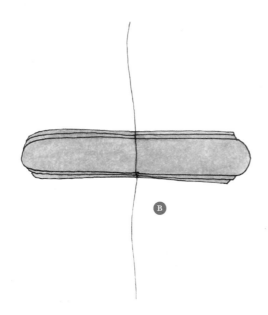

7. Lay the stack on its side and fan the stacks out in a circular shape C.

TIP: To add a special decorative touch, spray each pom-pom with glitter spray paint.

8. Beginning at the very middle, gently pull the innermost section of tissue paper layers straight out. Repeat this step as you move to the outer layers on both sides in a circular

Paper Ring Backdrop

Paper Ring Backdrop

DESIGNER: KATHRYN GODWIN

This paper ring backdrop is a one-of-a-kind piece that can be used for a ceremony backdrop, photo booth, or dessert table backdrop. Add color easily by spray painting, for a different look.

MATERIALS & TOOLS

- Watercolor paper
- Hot glue gun
- Hot glue sticks
- Twine or string
- Spray paint (optional)

Instructions

1. Tear strips of watercolor paper about 1 ½–2 ½ inches (3.8–6.3 cm) wide, and with lengths varying from 2–10 inches (5.1–25.4 cm), and a few that are 12–20 inches (30.5–50.8 cm).

2. Apply a line of hot glue along an end of a paper strip. Curve the paper to overlap the glue with the opposite end, creating a ring. Hold the ends in place while the glue sets. Repeat this step and create a variety of circle sizes.

3. Begin to create clusters of rings by applying a line of hot glue to one side of a circle, and pinch to join with another circle. Then apply a line of hot glue to both circles and join with a third.

4. Create large clusters of varying sizes, joining small circles around large circles. Create medium to large clusters. These can later be attached together on site, to allow for easier storage and transport.

5. When it is time to install the full piece, lay clusters out on the floor to create the shape of the full form. Apply lines of glue to any rings that will touch, and join the clusters together to create a larger shape.

TIP: To add spray paint, gently slide the backdrop onto a tarp. Spray the piece evenly with the paint and allow to dry before suspending the backdrop.

6. Tie twine to the top circles of the shape and double knot the twine to suspend the form.

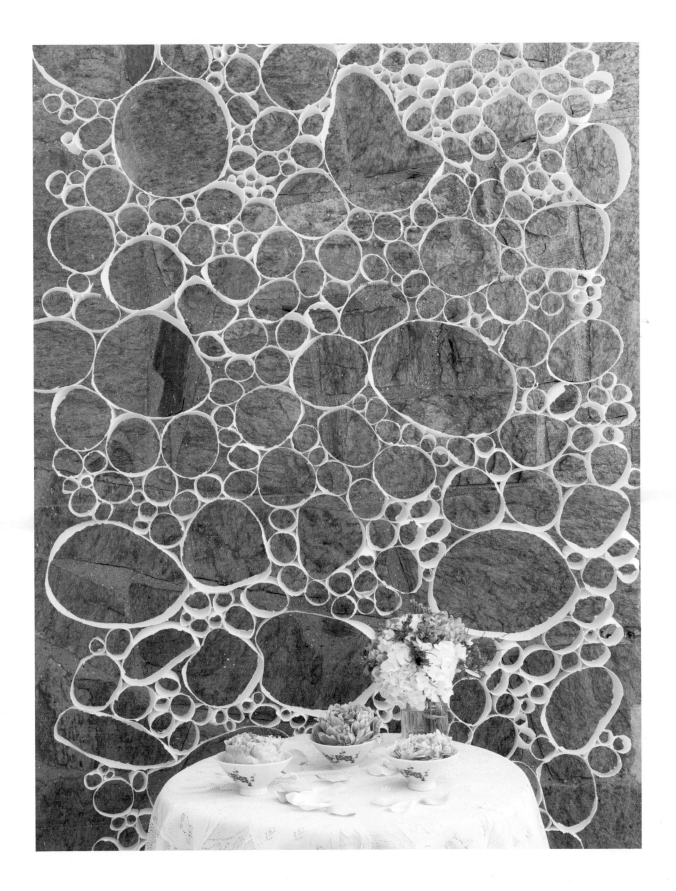

STATIONERY

THE PLEASURE OF YOUR COMPANY IS
REQUESTED AT THE MARRIAGE OF

Kimberly Rose Marini
to
Daniel Broderick

SATURDAY, SEPTEMBER 18TH
AT 5 O'CLOCK IN THE EVENING
123 PINE STREET
NEW YORK, NY 10000

Reception to follow

Paper-Cut Garden Vine Invitation

DESIGNER: BRITA VALLENS

This intricate paper-cut invitation features gracefully winding vines and beautiful flowers. Recipients of this card will feel doubly special when they receive an invitation that is not only beautiful, but handmade. Use a colored backing paper that matches your wedding's color scheme to give recipients of the invitations a sneak peek as to what they can expect to see on the big day.

MATERIALS & TOOLS

- Invitation design template (page 103)
- One sheet of regular copy paper
- One sheet of colored cardstock, at least 9 x 9 inches (22.8 x 22.8 cm)
- One sheet of white sketch paper
- Craft knife
- Metal ruler
- Cutting mat
- Craft glue
- Small, soft paintbrush
- Tape

Instructions

1. Copy the invitation design template onto regular copy paper. Cut the template outline from the copy paper and lay it over the white sketch paper. Use tape to affix the template to the sketch paper to keep it in place as you cut. Be sure to use a cutting mat to protect your work surface.

> **TIP:** If you've never used a craft knife before, practice working with the template, cardstock, craft knife, and cutting mat first.

2. Cut along the lines of the design template, using firm pressure to ensure that the blade is slicing through both the thin copy paper and the slightly heavier sketch paper. Take your time and be sure to keep your fingers away from the blade. You can rotate the paper as you go to make cutting in different directions easier. As you move from piece to piece, position the blade below the surface of the two layers of paper on the last cut to "pop" out the paper pieces.

3. When you finish cutting the entire template, gently move your hand over the copy paper to feel the grooves made by the blade to make sure you haven't missed any lines before removing the design template.

4. Lift the copy paper template from the sketch paper. If a few pieces of the cutout still remain, rescore the lines with your craft knife and gently pull the pieces out. Clean up any jagged or unclean lines with the blade of the craft knife.

5. Using a metal ruler to guide the craft knife, cut the colored cardstock backing 7¼ x 5 ¾ inches (18.4 x 14.6 cm).

6. Brush a thin layer of glue on the back of the paper cutting and affix it to the colored cardstock. Let the card dry, then place it beneath a stack of heavy books to ensure it lays flat.

Decorative Seating Cards

K & D

Kimberly Broderick
Table 8

Adams
le 3

Decorative Seating Cards

DESIGNER: BRITA VALLENS

Add a personal touch to your reception seating cards with colorful, decorative motifs made of tissue and craft papers to match your celebration's color scheme. Make any of the choices below, or use them as inspiration for your own one-of-a-kind design.

NOTE: Each card pictured is made using a 5 x 3½-inch (12.7 x 8.9 cm) notecard.

MATERIALS & TOOLS:

- Templates for cards A, B, C, and E (D does not have a template) (pages 104 and 105)

- Blank notecards, 5 x 3½ inches (12.7 x 8.9 cm) or sheets of cardstock, 5 x 7 inches (12.7 x 17.8 cm), folded in half

- Two sheets of cardstock: one patterned, the other solid green

- One sheet each of tissue paper in four colors (light pink, dark pink, yellow, and purple were used to make the cards shown)

- Scissors

- Craft knife

- Cutting mat

- Craft glue

- Black permanent marker

- Pencil

- Eraser

- Metal ruler

- Small, soft paintbrush

- Waxed paper

CARD A

1. Use the templates labeled "Card A" to create the two windows for this simple yet elegant card. Use a craft knife to cut the smaller window from tissue paper and the larger one from printed cardstock. Be sure to use a metal ruler to ensure neat, accurate cuts.

TIP: If you have never worked with a craft knife before, practice with the templates, paper, craft knife, and cutting mat first.

K & D

C

E

Adams
le 3

D

Kimberly Broderick
Table 8

B

Deborah Stack
Table 7

A

ett

2. Position the larger, outer (patterned) window piece first, making sure to center it on the front of the card. Use the soft paintbrush to brush craft glue on the back of the patterned craft paper and press the piece down on the card.

3. Brush a thin layer of craft glue on the note card in the shape of the inner smaller window piece made from the tissue paper. Press the tissue paper down on the front of the card, centered within the larger cardstock window.

4. Wait for the card to dry before placing it beneath a stack of heavy books to press the pieces flat.

TIP: Cover your cards with waxed paper before placing them under a stack of books if they are still wet. The waxed paper will prevent any wet glue from sticking to the book's cover.

CARD B

1. Copy the templates labeled "Card B" on to regular copy paper. Lay the piece of paper over the cardstock (patterned or solid), or tissue paper, as specified, to cut out the specified numbers of each template labeled "A," "B," "C," "D," and "E." Use the cutting mat to protect your work surface.

2. Arrange the five petal-shaped pieces of purple tissue paper (template "A") in place in each of the four corners of the card before gluing them down, to ensure that you have each of the 20 total petal pieces and their correct placement.

Starting at one corner, move the five pieces aside carefully so as not to crumple the delicate tissue paper, and brush a thin layer of craft glue onto the card. Place the middle, and longest, petal piece down first, brush a thin layer of glue on both sides of the petal before layering the next two side petal pieces down on either side. Repeat the process for the shortest pieces, which should be positioned at each end of the purple fan shape. Position each of the side pieces so they overlap the middle piece for a collage effect, resulting in light and dark shades of purple. Repeat this step for placement of the five purple tissue paper petal pieces at each corner of the place card.

3. Brush a thin layer of glue at a corner of the card and glue one piece "B" at the corner. Repeat this step to place each of the remaining "B" pieces at each corner of the card.

4. Brush a thin layer of glue at each corner of the card toward the bottom of each of the "B" pieces and add the final portion of the corner motif (piece "C") to each corner of the card.

5. Draw a thin line of glue along the top and bottom sections of the card between the corner motifs and add the two pieces of patterned cardstock, labeled "D" on page 105.

6. Draw a thin line of glue along the right and left sides of the card, between the corner motif pieces, and add the pieces of patterned cardstock labeled "Piece E."

7. Wait for the card to dry, then place it beneath a stack of heavy books to press the pieces flat.

CARD C

1. Copy the templates for "Card C" onto tracing paper, or regular copy paper. Transfer each of the flower templates to the tissue paper or patterned cardstock, then cut using the craft knife. Alternatively, lay the copy paper over the tissue paper or cardstock, and cut each piece using the template as a guide. Cut between five and ten pieces of each of the small, medium, and large flower template pieces. Be sure to use a cutting mat to protect your work surface.

2. Use a small, soft paintbrush to brush craft glue in a flower shape in the area on the place card where you would like to place the flower piece. (NOTE: The craft glue will dry clear, so as long as the glue is brushed on evenly, it won't be visible when dry.)

3. Place the tissue paper flower pieces first, then brush more glue on the surface of the tissue paper flower before adding a flower shape cut from the patterned cardstock.

4. Be playful with the placement of the flower pieces: Overlap the cardstock and the tissue paper flowers at skewed angles, or position the petals of individual flower pieces so they overlap. Varying the placement of the flowers from card to card will make them each unique and special.

TIP: Use a more generous amount of glue than usual for the cardstock pieces to ensure those heavier pieces stay in place.

---

5. Once the card is dry, use the permanent marker to draw small dots in the center of each flower. Place each card beneath a heavy stack of books to press the pieces flat.

CARD D

1. Use scissors or a craft knife to cut squares in different sizes from two or more shades of colored tissue paper.

2. Brush a generous amount of glue on one corner section of the card and place squares of different colors and sizes on the section. If you overlap the pieces, this will add an extra dimension of color from the shades created by the layered tissue paper. Use a bit extra glue where the pieces overlap, so the layers will stay together. Repeat this step for each corner section of the card. Make sure the middle of the card stays blank so there's space to write in the seating-placement name.

3. Once dry, place the card beneath a stack of heavy books to press the pieces flat.

CARD E

1. Using the templates provided, cut approximately 15–20 small, medium, and large petal pieces from the colored tissue paper. Lay the tissue paper over the copied template on top of a cutting mat and use a craft knife to cut the template pieces, or simply use scissors to cut each piece from the tissue paper.

2. Using a small, soft paintbrush, brush a thin layer of craft glue on the card where you would like to place each tissue paper petal. Be careful to use a minimal amount of glue so the pieces lay neat

and flat on the paper and the glue dries clear and smooth.

3. Overlap a small section of the petals at the edges as you lay the petals in the circle flower pattern. Carefully brush an additional thin layer of craft glue on the overlapping sections to saturate and darken the color of the overlapping tissue paper pieces.

4. Repeat steps 2 and 3 to affix each petal to the card as you create each flower. Be playful with the positioning of each flower: Overlap the petals of

a few, or use a variety of the small, medium, and large petals for an individual flower.

5. Use the leaf template to cut two leaves per flower from the green craft paper, then glue each to opposite sides of each flower on the card.

6. Allow the card to dry before using a permanent marker to draw black circles in the center of each flower.

7. Place the card beneath a stack of heavy books to press the pieces flat.

Vintage Wallpaper Envelope Seals

Vintage Wallpaper Envelope Seals

DESIGNER: VALERIE LLOYD

Add pretty accents to the outsides of invitations and thank-you notes with these heart-shaped vintage wallpaper seals. Look for wallpaper scraps or samples at flea markets, or source retro papers online. This project is so simple, yet it adds such character to plain envelopes. In a pinch, patterned scrapbook paper can be substituted for wallpaper.

MATERIALS & TOOLS

- Heart templates (page 106)
- Sealed invitation or thank-you note envelopes
- Selection of wallpaper scraps
- Pencil
- Scissors
- Glue stick
- Wax paper

Instructions

1. Select areas of the wallpaper that have interesting colors or patterns. Use a pencil to trace around the heart templates and cut the shapes out with scissors.

2. Lay the hearts facedown on a piece of wax paper, and use the glue stick to apply glue to the backs of them. Be sure to extend the glue all the way to the edges of the shapes.

3. Arrange one or two hearts glue-side down on the back of each sealed envelope, and press flat.

4. Sandwich the envelope between two sheets of wax paper, and place under a stack of books until the glue has dried. Repeat the process for each envelope.

ACCESSORIES

Recycled Book Page Flower
(Single Flower Variation)

DESIGNER: KIMBERLY BART

Recycle old books and give them a new life by making flowers to attach to gift boxes, napkin rings, place settings, and more. Make several single flowers to create a bouquet.

MATERIALS & TOOLS

- Five pages from a book, approximately 6 x 10 inches (15.2 x 25.4 cm)
- One 7-inch (17.8 cm) twist tie
- Scissors

Instructions

1. Lay five book pages evenly on top of one another.

2. Starting from the top end of the stacked book pages, make 1-inch folds until all the pages are folded into a zigzag shape.

3. Wrap the twist tie in the center of the folded paper and twist five times. Ⓐ

4. Cut each end of the paper into half-round petals at least 1-inch (2.5 cm) long.

5. Hold the folded paper by the twist tie, and start opening the flower one layer at a time. Pull from the center toward the tips, making sure to pull away from the twist tie. Ⓑ (Pulling solely on the tips may cause the paper to tear.) Continue pulling each layer away from the tie until you have completed one side. Now start on the second side.

DO NOT pull toward the tie, which would create a rounded pom rather than a flower.

6. Once both sides of the flower are open, start styling the flower. Pinch and pull the flower petals to fill in any holes. Cut any long petals that look out of place, rounding them with the scissors. Finish styling until the flower is complete.

Recycled Book Pom-Pom
Flower Bouquet

DESIGNER: KIMBERLY BART

Give your wedding vintage flair by creating a recycled book page bouquet. Use pages from the couple's favorite book to add a special personal touch.

MATERIALS **&** TOOLS

- Twenty-five pages from a book, approximately 6 x 10 inches (15.2 x 25.4 cm)
- Five 7-inch (17.8 cm) twist ties
- Scissors
- One 8 x 11-inch (20.3 x 27.4 cm) thin cardboard mailer
- Transparent tape
- Hot glue gun
- Hot glue sticks
- 48 inches (121.9 cm) of ¾-inch (1.9 cm) white satin ribbon

Instructions

1. Lay five book pages evenly on top of one another.

2. Starting from the top or bottom end of the stacked book pages, make 1-inch folds until all the pages are folded into a zigzag shape.

3. Using a twist tie, wrap the tie in the center of the folded paper and twist five times. (**NOTE:** Too few twists will allow the paper to unravel.) Ⓐ

4. Cut each end of the paper into half-round petals at least 1 inch (2.5 cm) long.

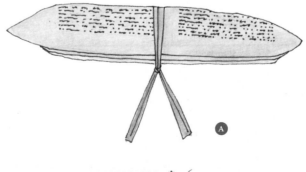

Ⓐ

5. Hold the folded paper by the twist tie, and start opening the flower one layer at a time **B**. Pull from the center toward the tips, making sure to pull away from the twist tie. (Pulling solely on the tips may cause the paper to tear.) Continue pulling each layer away from the tie until you have completed one side. Don't worry if small rips and tears occur while opening the flower. Now start on the second side. Do **NOT** pull toward the tie, which would create a rounded pom rather than a flower.

6. Once both sides of the flower are open, start styling the flower. Pinch and pull the flower petals to fill in any holes **C**. This is a good time to cut any long petals that look out of place, rounding them with the scissors. Once styling is complete, put the finished flower aside.

7. Repeat Steps 1–6 four more times to make a total of five flowers.

8. Gather the five completed flowers by their twist ties and hold them together in a bouquet. Twist all the ties together five times to hold the flowers in a group. Pull the twist ties straight out into a point. Set aside the group of five flowers.

9. Cut the thin cardboard mailer into a 7 x 9-inch (17.8 x 22.9 cm) sheet.

10. Roll the cardboard sheet into a cone with a 1½-inch (22.9 cm) opening at the top. Tape the cone so it stays rolled and keeps its shape.

11. Cut a 1-inch (2.5 cm) piece of ribbon and glue it to the bottom tip of the cone, covering the smaller hole.

12. Starting at the widest end, place a dab of glue near the top of the cone and place the ribbon over the glue.

13. Once the glue is set, start wrapping the ribbon around the cone, overlapping ¼ inch (.6 cm) over itself as you go.

14. Once one wraparound is complete, place a dab of glue on the ribbon and cone and continue gluing and wrapping until the entire cone is covered.

15. Neatly cut the end of the ribbon and glue to the cone. Allow the glue to set for five minutes.

16. Place a large amount of glue around the wide end of the cone. Stick the bouquet of paper flowers into the cone. Make sure the twist ties go into the cone and the cone is pushed all the way up against the base of the flower bouquet. Allow the bouquet to dry, then fluff the paper petals to complete.

Garden Rose Crepe Paper Crown

DESIGNER: VALERIE LLOYD

This lovely floral crown was inspired by heirloom rose gardens. It features lush, handmade crepe paper roses accented with wired leaves. The fanciful blooms are surprisingly simple to make, and can be made in any coordinating colors. The crown is tied at the back with romantic flowing ribbons.

MATERIALS & TOOLS

- Petal and leaf templates (page 107)
- Dark yellow crepe paper fold
- Scissors
- 24-gauge white floral wire
- White craft glue
- White floral tape
- Paintbrush
- Light yellow crepe paper fold
- 22-gauge white floral wire
- 1½ yards (1.4 m) ivory ribbon

Instructions

1. Use the leaf template to cut out two leaves from the dark yellow crepe paper. The grain should run with the length of the leaf shape. Paint a thin coat of white glue on one leaf; place a 5-inch (12.7 cm) length of 24-gauge floral wire along the center, lining it up with the tip of the leaf. Place the second leaf on top, and press flat. Let dry. Repeat the process to make four more leaves, each made up of two sides glued together with a wire running down the center. Once all five leaves are dry, bend the wire to give the leaves a naturalistic, curved shape.

2. Cut a 5 x ¾-inch (12.7 x 1.9 cm) rectangle of dark yellow crepe paper, with the grain of the paper running against the length. Cut a fringe along the entire length of the strip, with each cut going about one third of the way through the width. The simplest way to do this is to fold the strip several times, so you can cut through multiple layers at once. Take a 5-inch (12.7 cm) length of 24-gauge floral wire, and dip just the end in white glue. Attach the end of the fringe strip, and wrap it around the wire. Seal the end of the fringe strip with glue. Ruffle the fringe outward so it looks somewhat like the bristles of a paintbrush (A).

3. Use the petal template to cut out ten petals from the light yellow crepe paper, with the grain of the paper running with the length. Gently stretch the centers of each petal outward to form a slightly cupped shape. (NOTE: Do not stretch the tops of the petals, just the centers.) Dab a very small amount of glue on the bottom point of a petal, and attach it to the wire stem, just under the fringe B . Add the second petal, placing it slightly overlapping the first. Continue adding petals one by one, attaching them with glue at the bases. When the flower has ten petals, use a short strip of white floral tape to wrap the bases of all the petals tightly against the wire stem. Cut one ½-inch (1.2 cm) wide strip of dark yellow crepe paper off the end of the fold. Use it to cover the floral tape. Repeat the process to make a second flower.

4. Cut an 18-inch (45.72 cm) length of 22-gauge floral wire, and bend it into a horseshoe shape, to be used as the headband. Gather three leaves from Step 1, fan them out, and bind their stems together with the floral tape. Add one flower, and bind its stem to the leaves. Use floral tape to apply the flower and leaves to the headband, just off to one side. Gather the remaining flower and leaves, bind their stems together, and apply them to the headband, just under the others. Arrange the flowers so that they are side by side.

5. Use floral tape to cover the rest of the headband wire so that it is all a uniform thickness. Cut a ½-inch (1.2 cm) strip of dark yellow crepe paper off the end of the fold, and use it to cover any visible floral tape C . Seal the ends of the paper strip with dots of glue. Bend the ends of the headband wire up into small loops, and tie ribbons to the ends.

Boutonniere & Corsage

DESIGNER: KATHRYN GODWIN

No need to worry about any wilting flowers on this beautiful floral corsage and boutonniere. The flowers are made using dyed coffee filters. Make these for a special (and lasting) twist on traditional boutonnieres and corsages for members of the wedding party.

MATERIALS & TOOLS

- Small coffee filters
- Petal templates (pages 108 and 109)
- Leaf templates (page 108)
- Fabric dye
- Green cardstock or scrapbook paper
- Green cloth–covered floral wire
- Hot glue gun

- Hot glue sticks
- 30 inches of ½-inch (1.2 cm) satin ribbon
- 15 inches of ¼-inch (0.6 cm) satin ribbon
- Scissors
- Wire cutters
- Pliers

Instructions for Making the Flowers

In a large bowl, mix the fabric dye with water and follow the instructions on the fabric dye packet. The more water you add to the dye, the lighter the colors will be. The colors can be mixed to create different hues—orange and fuchsia mix to create a coral shade. Have fun playing with the varieties that can be created! Quickly dip the coffee filter into the dye bath and set aside to dry.

OVAL PETAL PAPER FLOWERS

1. Choose a colored filter for the center of the oval petal flower, and fold it in half three times. Cut to 1½ inch (3.81 cm) size, and fringe the edge with scissors Ⓐ.

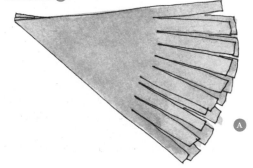

2. Unfold the filter and pierce through its center with a 3-inch (7.6 cm) length of the floral wire. Apply a bead of glue around the center of the coffee filter and pinch around the floral wire ⓑ.

3. Use the petal template to cut the petal shapes from a dyed coffee filter. There will be sixteen oval-tipped petals for each flower.

4. Apply a dot of hot glue to the bottom of each petal, then pinch around the base of the fringed center. Attach four petals for the first layer, at opposite sides of the center. For the second layer, attach four more to fill in the spaces between each petal of the first layer. Continue to do so until you have four layers with four petals each ⓒ.

CHRYSANTHEMUM PAPER FLOWERS

1. To create a paper chrysanthemum, fold a dyed coffee filter in half three times. Use the petal template to cut the petals from the dyed coffee filter.

2. Unfold the cut filter and then loosely refold, intentionally misaligning the petals. Fold it into quarters. Fold the point up toward the petals twice ⓓ, and then begin to roll the right petals toward and into the left ⓔ.

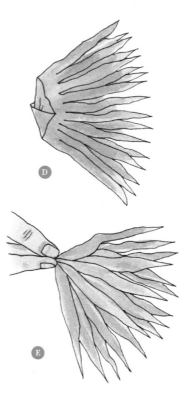

3. Apply hot glue and pinch around the floral wire, circling with the petals. If any petals appear too long or misplaced, gently pull and fluff appropriately; trim where needed to create a consistent length and shape.

INSTRUCTIONS FOR MAKING THE CORSAGE

1. To create the corsage, use two oval petal flowers and one chrysanthemum. With pliers, grip the wire at the base of the flower and gently press the flower to bend at a 90-degree angle.

2. Holding the two flowers together, begin to twist wires around each of them in a straight line. Pull a third flower in to sandwich the chrysanthemum and twist its wire in the opposite direction around the previously formed line of wire Ⓐ.

Ⓐ

3. Curve the ends of the wire into an oval shape like a bracelet cuff. Trim the ends of the wire so they are even.

4. Using the leaf templates, cut leaves from the green paper, then fold the leaves in half lengthwise to create dimension. Attach the leaves with hot glue to the underside of the wire structure, overlapping at slight angles. Before gluing the final leaves, hold them in place to check appropriate paper color, and if necessary, trim away parts of the leaf base to allow for them to tuck smoothly into place alongside the other leaves and the wire form.

5. To finish the corsage, apply a dot of hot glue at one end of the wire cuff. Fold ½-inch (1.27 cm) piece of satin ribbon around the wire end and begin to wrap it around to cover the full cuff. Finish off the opposite end by trimming the ribbon and folding the cut edge under and tacking it with glue. The wire cuff can be moved and formed to fit any size wrist.

6. Cut a 20-inch (50 cm) length of ½ inch (1.2 cm) satin ribbon and tie it in a bow. Attach it to the cuff, under the leaves, with hot glue. Trim the ends to your preferred length.

TO MAKE THE BOUTONNIERE

1. To make a boutonniere, select a paper flower and bend it slightly at the base to create an angle from the straight stem. It does not need to be as severe an angle as was created for the corsage.

2. Using the leaf template, cut green cardstock to size and fold the leaf in half to create a center vein. Attach two leaves together with hot glue at a slight angle to each other to create the backside of the

Ⓑ

flower and stem . Attach a third leaf to the front, underside of the flower that is opposite to the direction of the leaves on the backside.

3. Cut a wire stem 2 inches (5.1 cm) in length. Dot the wire with hot glue and fold a ¼-inch (.6 cm) piece of satin ribbon around the end of the wire, and then wrap up toward the flower. Cut the end and glue it in place.

4. Cut a 10-inch (25 cm) length of ¼-inch (.6 cm) satin ribbon and tie it in a bow. Attach it to the front underside of the flower with a dot of hot glue.

TIP: The flowers can be dyed to match any wedding color scheme.

Starburst Cake Topper

Starburst Cake Topper

DESIGNER: BRITA VALLENS

This elegant, shimmering, Art Deco–inspired cake topper adds an extra layer of personalized charm to the reception festivities. For an extra special touch, add the couple's initials, their full names, or a picture to the center of the cake topper.

MATERIALS & TOOLS

- Starburst template (page 110)
- One sheet of white cardstock, at least 4 x 4 inches (10.2 x 10.2 cm)
- One sheet of colored cardstock in the color of your choice for the starburst, at least 10 x 10 inches (25.4 x 25.4 cm)
- Craft glue
- Hot glue gun
- Hot glue sticks
- Wooden skewer or craft stick

- Craft knife
- Cutting mat
- Metal ruler
- Glitter
- Tape
- Large circle squeeze punch, 2 inches (5.1 cm) in diameter (or a compass and scissors)
- Small, soft paintbrush
- Calligraphy pen (optional)

Instructions

1. Copy the starburst template onto regular copy paper. Place the copy over the colored cardstock and tape in place.

TIP: If you've never used a craft knife before, practice working with the template, cardstock, craft knife, and cutting mat first.

2. Using the craft knife and metal ruler, cut along the lines of the template. Press down firmly as you cut, and take your time to avoid cutting mistakes. Start at the center of the design and move outward as you cut along each line.

3. When the entire template has been cut, remove it from the cardstock: Carefully bend the cardstock to check if any cuts need

to be redone to ensure the design will pull away cleanly. Use the metal ruler to carefully recut along any shallow lines and clean up any jagged edges with the blade of your craft knife.

4. Pull the starburst away from the cardstock, and remove the interior pieces to reveal the final shape.

5. On the front side of the starburst (you choose which is the front), use the paintbrush to evenly apply a thin layer of glue on the tip of each of the star's points, then sprinkle glitter over the glue. Shake off any excess glitter.

6. Punch a circle 2 inches (5.1 cm) in diameter from the white cardstock using the large squeeze punch. Or, you can use a compass to inscribe the circle and cut it out with scissors.

7. Next, write the couple's initials or full names on the circle with a calligraphy pen. You may need to try a few times until you are satisfied with the writing.

TIP: You can also place a picture of the couple on the center of the starburst.

8. Glue the circle to the center of the starburst with craft glue.

9. Let the starburst dry, then place it under some heavy books to ensure it lays flat.

10. Cut a ½ x 2-inch (1.2 x 5.1cm) rectangle from the white cardstock. Use a glue gun to apply a line of glue down the back of the starburst and glue the wooden stick down. Add a few dots of glue across and on either side of the stick in the middle of the circle and lay the rectangle of cardstock across the stick for extra stability A.

Giant Paper Daisies

Giant Paper Daisies

DESIGNER: VALERIE LLOYD

These giant daisies make whimsical bouquet alternatives for bridesmaids or flower girls. Stake them in the ground to decorate an outdoor space, or use them as playful props for a photo booth. They are irresistibly fun, and are a great way to add color and character to the celebration.

MATERIALS & TOOLS

- Petal template (page 111)
- Calyx template (page 112)
- Two sheets of yellow tissue paper
- Scissors
- Three sheets of white cardstock
- Hot glue gun

- Low temp hot glue sticks
- 15–18 yellow chenille stems
- 18-inch (45.7 cm) wooden dowel
- 22-gauge floral wire
- Green crepe paper fold
- Masking tape

Instructions

1. Cut out a circle of cardstock approximately 7 inches (17. 8 cm) in diameter. Use the petal template to cut out thirty petals from the yellow tissue paper. Gather and pinch the bases of each petal to create a boatlike shape .

2. Begin making the flower by applying petals to the back of the cardstock circle. Apply a

dot of hot glue to the base of a petal, and press it onto the cardstock circle with the rounded side of the petal facing up. Let about ⅔ of the petal extend beyond the edge of the circle. Lift the tip of the petal, and apply a second dot of glue to the edge of the circle. Press the petal back down so that it is attached to the cardstock in two spots. Continue adding more petals all the way around the cardstock circle.

3. Turn the flower over, and begin adding a row of petals around the front edge of the circle. This time, apply the glue to the other side of the petals, so that the rounded side is facing down when placed onto the cardstock. Line the tips of the petals up with the petals on the back of the flower. Once the row is complete, add another row of petals, gluing their bases to the previous row. For this row, place them slightly closer to the center of the flower.

4. Cut out a circle of cardstock approximately 4 inches (10.1 cm) in diameter. Coil each chenille stem into a tight spiral shape, and tuck the ends of the stems underneath the coil. Use hot glue to apply the chenille coils to the cardstock circle: Start at the edges, and work toward the center, overlapping the coils if necessary. Let the coils extend over the edges slightly so that all of the cardstock is covered. Apply a generous amount of hot glue to the back of the circle, and press it into the center of the flower.

5. Attach the head of the flower with a wire joint, to allow the angle of the flower to be adjusted: Cut two 9-inch (22.9 cm) lengths of floral wire. Hold

the floral wires together, and bend them in half to make a single loop shape. Use a length of masking tape to bind the ends of the wires to the end of the wooden dowel B. The looped end of the wire should extend about 2 inches (5.1 cm) past the end of the dowel. Cut a circle of cardstock ~4 inches (10.1 cm) in diameter. Use the point of the scissors to poke a hole in the center of the circle. Insert the wire loop through the hole using two pieces of masking tape to attach it to the cardstock circle C.

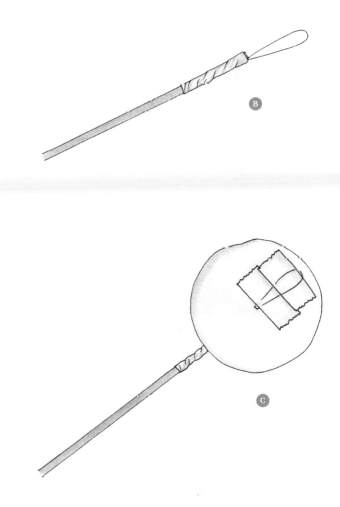

6. Cut a 4-inch (10.1 cm) section off the end of the green crepe paper fold. Unfold it to create a long strip. Apply hot glue to the end of the strip, and press it to the top of the wooden dowel over the masking tape. Twist the dowel while holding the paper strip taut, until it is entirely covered with the green crepe paper. Seal the end of the paper with hot glue at the base of the dowel.

7. Apply a generous amount of hot glue to the cardstock circle at the top of the dowel, and press it to the back of the flower. Cut the calyx template from the green crepe paper. Use the point of the scissors to poke a hole in the center of the calyx; then slide it up over the dowel. Attach it to the cardstock on the back of the circle with glue. Wrap one more 4-inch (10.1 cm) strip of the green crepe paper to thicken the upper part of the flower's stem 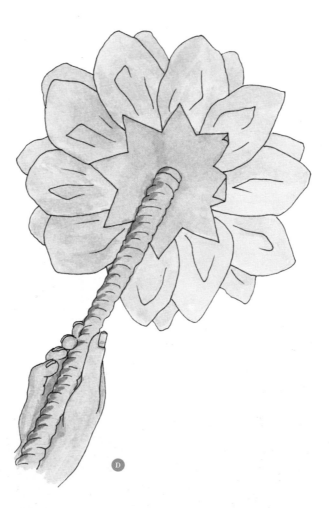.

Box It Up! Favor Boxes

DESIGNER: SANDI GENOVESE

The beauty of making your own wedding favors is the degree to which you can personalize them so that they reflect the bride and groom and help to set the mood for their special day.

MATERIALS & TOOLS

- Flower template (page 113)
- Recycled box or box template (page 114)
- Transparent or washi tape to match flower paper
- Brads in coordinating colors

- $\frac{1}{8}$-or $\frac{1}{16}$-inch hole punch
- Scrapbook paper or cardstock to match the wedding color palette
- Small colored candies in two different colors
- Adhesive of choice

Instructions

CREATE THE 3-D FLOWER

1. Using the template provided, hand cut five (or more) flowers from cardstock A.

2. Fold two flowers in half and glue them to a 1¾ inch (4.5 cm) square cut from complementary cardstock to form the base. Punch a small hole in the center of the square in the middle of the cardstock base.

A

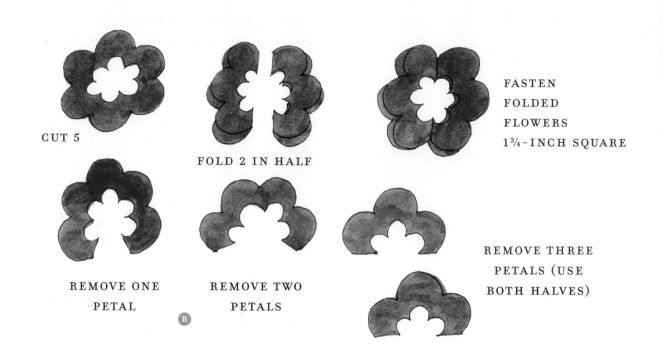

CUT 5

FOLD 2 IN HALF

FASTEN
FOLDED
FLOWERS
1¾-INCH SQUARE

REMOVE ONE
PETAL

REMOVE TWO
PETALS

REMOVE THREE
PETALS (USE
BOTH HALVES)

B

3. Cut out and remove one petal from a cardstock flower. Remove two petals from the next flower and remove three petals from the last flower B. (You will use both halves.)

4. Pull the two ends of the petals together on each flower and fasten them together with transparent tape or a matching piece of washi tape.

5. Fasten each 3-D flower to the base (with the largest on the bottom) with glue dots or a glue gun. Curl the final flower a bit tighter than the previous layer before attaching the ends together with tape.

6. Finish the flower with a patterned brad attached through the hole in the middle of the square base.

CREATE THE BOX

OPTION 1: Use the box template provided to cut out a box. Cut on the solid lines and fold on the dotted lines. Place adhesive on the tab to assemble.

OPTION 2: Dismantle a box and use it as a template.

OPTION 3: Recycle a small box and cover the sides and top with paper to match the wedding color palette.

TIP: Personalize by hand-writing the couple's names diagonally across the paper covering the box lid.

Attach the flower to the lid with an aggressive adhesive such as hot glue, or glue dots.

FILL THE BOX

1. Cut a strip of scrapbook paper or cardstock that is a little narrower than the height of the box. Fold the strip in half.

2. Place a strong adhesive on one end of the strip and curl the two ends so they touch and form a heart shape that fits inside the box.

3. Place the heart inside the box. Pour one color of candy inside the heart and a different color of candy outside the heart.

TEMPLATES

The following templates can be printed at full size on 8½ x 11-inch paper (unless otherwise noted). Please be sure to set your printer to "actual size" or "size to 100%." Do not select the "to fit" setting.

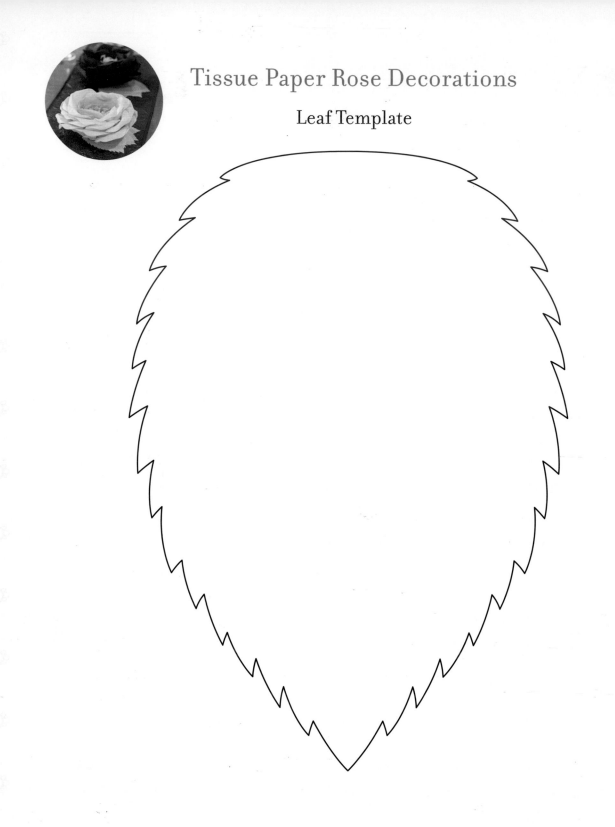

Tissue Paper Rose Decorations

Leaf Template

Actual Size

Tissue Paper Rose Decorations

Petal Template

Actual Size

Cascading Butterflies

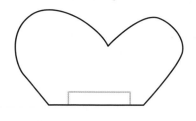

Small

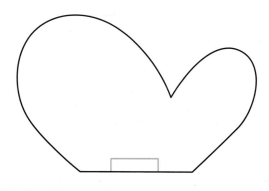

Medium

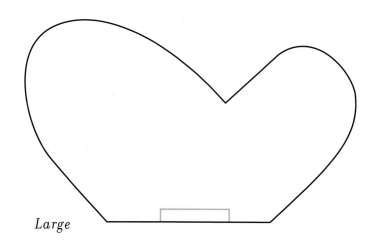

Large

Actual Sizes

Vellum-Cut Window Lantern

Lantern Body Template

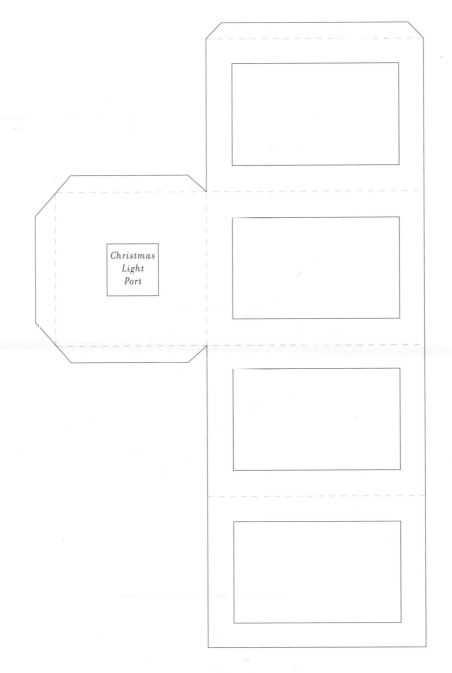

*Christmas
Light
Port*

Enlarge to 285%

Vellum-Cut Window Lantern
Window Design Template

Actual Size

Paper Flower Branch

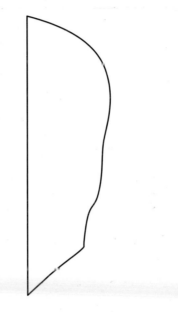

Actual Size

Heart-Shaped 3-D Decoration

Enlarge to 330%

Paper Ball Backdrop

Enlarge to 185%

Paper Leaf Garland

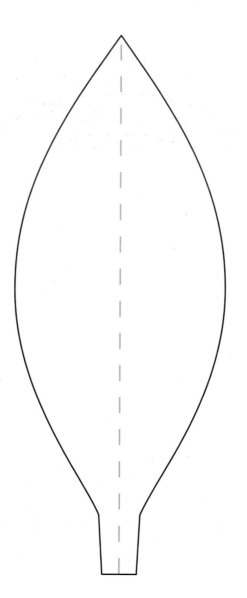

Actual Size

Paper-Cut Garden Vine Invitation

Actual Size

Decorative Seating Cards

Actual Size

Decorative Seating Cards

CARD B

A) *Tissue Paper (Cut 20)*

B) *(Cut 4)*

C) *(Cut 4)*

D) *(Cut 2)*

E) *(Cut 2)*

CARD C

Medium

Small

CARD E

Large   Petals   Small

Medium

Leaves

Actual Size

Actual Size

Garden Rose Crepe Paper Crown

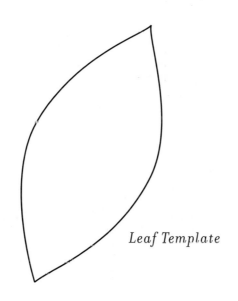

Leaf Template

Petal Template

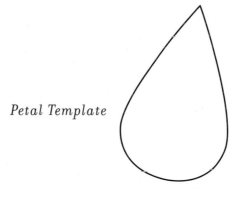

Actual Size

Boutonniere & Corsage

Leaves

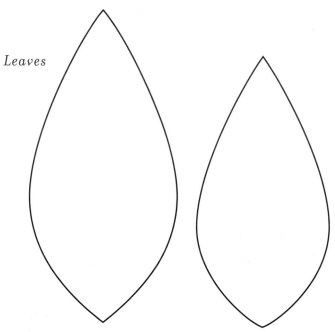

Oval Petals

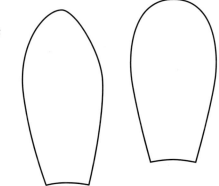

Actual Sizes

Boutonniere & Corsage

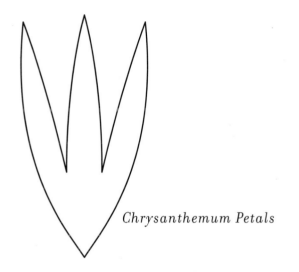

Chrysanthemum Petals

Oval Petal Flower Center

Actual Sizes

Starburst Cake Topper

Actual Size

Giant Paper Daisies

Petal Template

Actual Size

Giant Paper Daisies

Calyx Template

Actual Size

Box It Up! Favor Boxes

Flower Template

Actual Size

Box It Up! Favor Boxes

Box Template

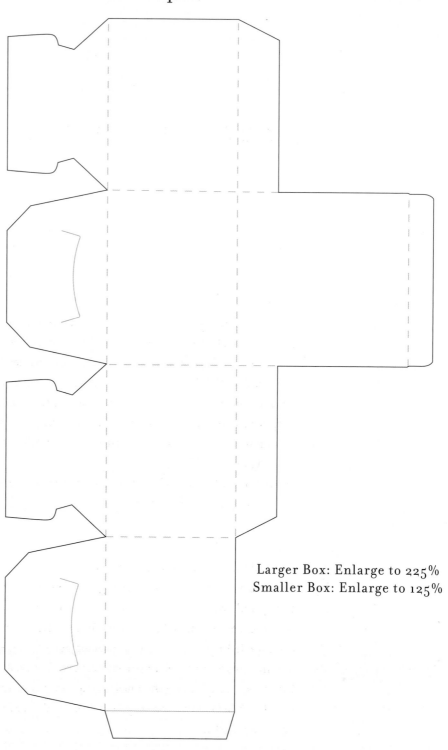

Larger Box: Enlarge to 225%
Smaller Box: Enlarge to 125%

ABOUT THE DESIGNERS

KIMBERLY BART

Kimberly Bart is a successful entrepreneur, author, podcaster, designer, wife, and mother. She started her career in graphic design and ran her own studio, creating innovative packaging designs for leading companies including Disney, LeapFrog, Sega, and Mattel. She later shifted her creative focus to build a successful interior design company. More recently, she has built a string of successful online businesses out of her desire to spend more time with her daughter. When she is not with her family on the deck of her floating home in Portland, Oregon, she can be found creating new products for her business, interviewing new artists for her podcast, and helping others establish their own successful online ventures. You can find her at www.handmadeprofits.com.

JESSICA FEDIW

As a military wife and devoted mother of two, Jessica has traveled throughout the East Coast and Gulf states, splitting her time and energy between raising a young family and channeling her creative passions. Early on, Jessica began sewing as a way to make one-of-a-kind outfits for her daughter. She took to blogging online and founded Happy Together (www.happytogetherbyjess.com) to capture her journey and share her experiences with others. Eventually, she expanded her creative interests to much more than just sewing. Jessica is influencing others around the world with her genuine message that love, family, and happiness are found when we share life together.

SANDI GENOVESE

Sandi has authored several craft books and has shared her creations as a guest on several television shows such as *GOOD MORNING AMERICA* and *THE VIEW* as well as her own TV show, which aired on the DIY and HGTV networks. She licenses her designs with several companies, including her own product line, the Sandi G Collection, for HSN. You can enjoy her creations through videos which are posted weekly on her website, sandigenovese.com.

KATHRYN GODWIN

Kathryn Godwin is an innovative installation artist and cultivator of community. Having grown up in Florida, she received her BFA in Studio Art from Florida State University, and now calls North Carolina home. Individuals, retailers, and companies have incorporated her large-scale and intricate art pieces in store openings, celebrations, and media across the country and world. Kathryn is known for working with a number of materials—both traditional and unexpected—and she challenges conventional studio art to create playful, whimsical, and accessible pieces that offer a sense of place and time. Clients include the Biltmore Estate, Off Broadway Shoes, Anthropologie, BHLDN, and Belk.

VALERIE LLOYD

Valerie Lloyd is no stranger to glittery messes and hot glue "situations." After achieving success with her Etsy shop, Smile Mercantile, Valerie launched smile-mercantile.com, where she sells specialty craft supplies and seasonal decorations. When not crafting up a storm, she enjoys photography, tending her garden, or hunting for vintage treasures at thrift stores and estate sales. Valerie lives in Seattle with her husband, Khris, and their cat, Bentley.

BRITA VALLENS

Brita Vallens is an editor at Lark Crafts. She loves to doodle and craft—especially with paper. Give her a piece of paper and a pen, and she'll happily doodle away for hours. Most recently, she has been experimenting with "doodle cut-outs" by cutting intricate designs out of paper using a craft knife. To learn more about Brita and see what she is currently working on, visit larkcrafts.com.

RESOURCES

Part of the fun in making papercrafts is shopping for the materials. You can't help but be inspired as you peruse your local paper shop or papercraft website—so many options, so many beautiful patterns and textures! Here are a few of our favorite paper craft stores and their websites:

Paper Source™/www.papersource.com

Paper Presentation™/www.paperpresentation.com

Kate's Paperie™/www.katespaperie.com

Michaels™/www.michaels.com

Jo-Ann Fabric and Craft Stores™/www.joann.com

INDEX